Stories from Islam

A Handsome Young Man

Ziya Us Salam

Om KIDZ

An imprint of Om Books International

Prophet Yusuf was a very handsome man. His good-looks enchanted people. Salman secretly wanted to be good-looking, too.

Every time he wore a new shirt, he stood in front of the mirror, and imagined himself to be very handsome and admired by all. One day, he asked his grandmother to tell him the story of Prophet Yusuf.

"I have told you this story a hundred times, Salman," Rasheeda complained, but gave in as Salman continued to insist, "Grandma, just one more time, please."

"All right, then," Rasheeda said, "Let us begin. Prophet Yusuf had an unusual life. He lived in the kingdom of an evil Pharaoh, in the house of one of the Pharaoh's ministers.

"The minister had a wicked wife who liked to spread lies. She liked Prophet Yusuf and wanted to marry him. Prophet Yusuf asked her to be loyal to her husband, a kind man. He did not want to betray her husband's trust. He had given shelter to Prophet Yusuf in his time of need.

"However, as Prophet Yusuf did not listen to the minister's evil wife, she had her husband send Prophet Yusuf to prison."

"But that was not the end!" Salman smiled as his grandmother had reached his favourite part of the story.

"We plan, Salman, but the best planner is Allah," Rasheeda said. "Prophet Yusuf was sent to prison, but became famous as he could understand people's dreams. His fame spread quickly.

“The Pharaoh also heard of him. Once the Pharaoh saw a dream, and wanted Prophet Yusuf to tell him its meaning. Prophet Yusuf was still in prison and could not come out.

"When the Pharaoh decided to find out the truth, it was revealed that Prophet Yusuf had been charged wrongly, and so the Pharaoh declared him innocent."

"Did Prophet Yusuf understand the Pharaoh's dream?" Salman asked.

Rasheeda nodded. “Yes, Salman, he did. The Pharaoh had a dream in which he saw seven skinny cows eating seven well-fed ones. He also saw seven plump ears of wheat along with seven lean ones. Prophet Yusuf explained the dream to the Pharaoh.

"He told the Pharaoh that there would be seven years of prosperity in his kingdom, followed by seven years of famine; when people would not have much to eat. After that would come a year of plentiful rain.

"The Pharaoh was impressed with Prophet Yusuf's understanding of his dream. He made Prophet Yusuf in charge of the store houses to ensure that there was enough stock of wheat for any bad years they might have in the future."

"He was such a wise man," said Salman, his voice dreamy with wonder. Rasheeda agreed. "That he was. You must learn to be just and honest, and follow your dreams," Rasheeda told her grandson. With this advice, Rasheeda ended the story.